HEART THOUGHTS

Also by Louise L. Hay

All of the above are available at your local bookstore, or may be ordered by visiting:

Hay House USA: www.hayhouse.com®; Hay House Australia: www.hayhouse.com.au; Hay House; UK: www.hayhouse.co.uk;
Hay House South Africa: www.hayhouse.co.za; Hay House India: www.hayhouse.co.in

HEART
THOUGHTS

A Treasury of Inner Wisdom

LOUISE L. HAY

HAY HOUSE, INC.
Carlsbad, California • New York City
London • Sydney • Johannesburg
Vancouver • Hong Kong • New Delhi

Published and distributed in the United States by: Hay House, Inc.: www.hayhouse.com • *Published and distributed in Australia by:* Hay House Australia Pty. Ltd.: www.hayhouse.com.au • *Published and distributed in the United Kingdom by:* Hay House UK, Ltd.: www.hayhouse.co.uk • *Published and distributed in the Republic of South Africa by:* Hay House SA (Pty), Ltd.: www .hayhouse.co.za • *Distributed in Canada by:* Raincoast: www.raincoast.com • *Published in India by:* Hay House Publishers India: www.hayhouse.co.in

Editorial supervision: Jill Kramer   •   *Editorial assistant:* Nicolette Salamanca
Cover design: Katie Daisy   •   *Interior design:* Charles McStravick
Interior illustrations: Katie Daisy

Originally published in a traditional format in December 1991, by Hay House, Inc.: ISBN: 978-1-56170-045-5

Library of Congress Control Number: 2011929973

ISBN: 978-1-4019-3720-1

15 14 13 12   6 5 4 3
1st (gift) edition, February 2012
3rd edition, August 2012

Printed in China

Dedicated to your heart.

Your heart is the center of your power.
I have learned that you can create easily
and effortlessly when you let your thoughts
come from the loving space of the heart.

Claim your power now.

Contents

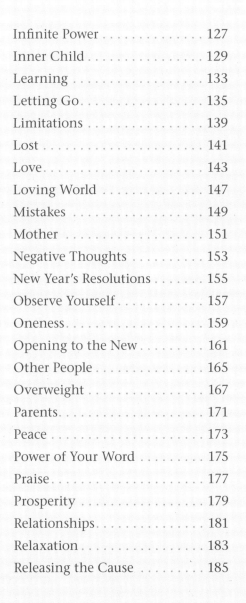

Introduction

This book is a combination of meditations, spiritual treatments, and excerpts from my lectures. It focuses on aspects of our day-to-day experiences and is meant to guide and assist us in particular areas where we may be having difficulty.

When we feel like victims, we tend to isolate ourselves. We feel pain and fear, and we are always looking for someone else to save us, to do it for us. We now have an opportunity to discover our abilities to re-spond to Life—not as victims, but in ways that give us power. We will find that as we start to connect with what I call the *Inner Self*, we can contribute to improving the quality of our lives. It is a fantastic feeling to know that we don't have to be dependent on someone else, but that we have within us a tremendous capacity to make positive changes in our lives. It is wonderfully liberating.

Some people may be frightened by this new liberation because it seems like *responsibility*. But responsibility merely means that we are able to respond to Life. We are moving into a new age and a new order. It is time for us to release old beliefs and old habits. As we continue to learn and practice new beliefs and new methods of behavior, we will contribute harmoniously to the new order of the world.

Be patient with yourself. From the moment you decide to make a change until you see the results of your efforts, you may vacillate from the old to the new. Don't get angry with yourself. You want to *build* yourself up, not *beat* yourself up. You may wish to refer to this book during those times when you are "in between" the old and the new, using the meditations and treatments on a daily basis until you build your confidence in your capability to make changes.

This is a time of awakening. Know that you are always safe. It may not seem so at first, but you will learn that Life is always there for you. Know that it is possible to move from the old order into the new order safely and peacefully.

I love you,

Louise L. Hay

The more we dwell

on what we *don't* want,

the more we get exactly that.

By focusing on what we *do* want,

we attract abundance and

other good things.

I AM A YES PERSON

I know that I am one with all of Life. I am surrounded and permeated with Infinite Wisdom. Therefore, I rely totally on the Universe to support me in every positive way. Everything I could possibly need is already here waiting for me. This planet has more food on it than I could possibly eat. There is more money than I could ever spend. There are more people than I could ever meet. There is more love than I could possibly experience. There is more joy than I can even imagine. This world has everything I need and desire. It is all mine to use and to have.

The One Infinite Mind, the One Infinite Intelligence, always says *yes* to me. No matter what I choose to believe or think or say, the Universe always says *yes*. I do not waste my time on negative thinking or negative subjects. I choose to see myself and Life in the most positive ways. As such, I say *yes* to opportunity and prosperity. I say *yes* to all good. I am a *yes* person living in a *yes* world, being responded to by a *yes* Universe; and I rejoice that this is so. I am grateful to be one with Universal Wisdom and backed by Universal Power. Thank you, God, for all that is mine to enjoy in the here and now.

Look in the mirror and say:

"I love and accept myself

exactly as I am."

What comes up in your mind?

Notice how you feel.

This may be the center

of your problem.

I ACCEPT ALL PARTS OF MYSELF

The biggest part of healing or making ourselves whole is to accept all of the many parts of ourselves. The times when we did well, and the times when we didn't do so well. The times when we were terrified, and the times when we were loving. The times when we were very foolish and silly, and the times when we were very bright and clever. The times when we had egg on our faces, and the times when we were winners. All of these are parts of ourselves.

Most of our problems stem from rejecting parts of ourselves—not loving ourselves totally and unconditionally. Let's not look back on our lives with shame. Look at the past as the richness and fullness of Life. Without this richness and fullness, we would not be here today. When we accept all of ourselves, we become whole and healed.

If you do not love yourself

totally, wholly, and fully,

somewhere along the way

you learned not to.

You can unlearn it.

Start being kind

to yourself now.

I ACCEPT ALL THAT I HAVE CREATED FOR MYSELF

I love and accept myself exactly as I am. I support myself, trust myself, and accept myself wherever I am. I can be within the love of my own heart. I place my hand over my heart and feel the love that is there. I know there is plenty of room for me to accept myself right here and now. I accept my body, my weight, my height, my appearance, my sexuality, and my experiences. I accept all that I have created for myself—my past and my present. I am willing to allow my future to happen. I am a Divine, Magnificent Expression of Life, and I deserve the very best. I accept this for myself now. I accept miracles. I accept healing. I accept wholeness. And most of all, I accept myself. I am precious, and I cherish who I am. And so it is.

We create certain situations,

such as accidents, and then we

give our power away by blaming others

for our frustrations.

No person, place, or thing

has any power over us.

We are the only thinkers

in our minds.

I EXPRESS MYSELF IN POSITIVE WAYS

Usually if you are in an accident, and you are the one who is hit, you feel guilt on a deep level and perhaps have a need for punishment. There can be a lot of repressed hostility—the feeling that you do not have the right to speak up for yourself. If you hit somebody, you are often dealing with unexpressed anger. This gives you an opportunity to express that anger. There is always more "stuff" going on inside you. An accident is more than an accident. When one occurs, look within to see your own pattern, bless the other person with love, and then release the entire experience.

The moment you say affirmations,

you are stepping out

of the victim role.

You are no longer helpless.

You are acknowledging

your own power.

I AM ON THE NEXT STEP TO MY HEALING

An affirmation is a beginning point. It opens the way. You are saying to your subconscious mind: "I am taking responsibility. I am aware there is something I can do to change." If you continue to say the affirmation, either you will be ready to let whatever it is go and the affirmation will come true, or it will open a new avenue to you. You may get a brilliant brainstorm, or a friend may call you and ask, "Have you ever tried this?" You will be led to the next step that will help you with your healing.

Affirmations give
your subconscious mind
something to work on
in the moment.

I AM OPEN AND RECEPTIVE

If we do affirmations to create good in our lives but there's a part of us that doesn't believe we are worth it, we are not going to manifest those affirmations. We will get to the point when we say, "Affirmations don't work."

The truth is, it has nothing to do with the affirmations; it's that we don't believe we are deserving.

We must become aware of what

we believe about ourselves.

By doing so, we can change

those beliefs that are

not serving us.

THE ANSWERS WITHIN ME COME TO MY AWARENESS WITH EASE

If you're doing your affirmations in front of a mirror, always have a pad and pencil handy so you can write down the negative messages that come to mind when you say them. You don't have to deal with the information right then. Later you can sit down and look at what you wrote, and if there is a list of negative responses, you can begin to understand why you don't have what you say you want. If you are not aware of your negative messages, it is very difficult to change them.

Every time you get angry,

you're affirming that you want

more anger in your life.

ANGER IS A DEFENSE MECHANISM

Anger is a normal and natural process. Usually you get angry about the same things over and over again. When you're angry, you feel that you don't have a right to express it, so you swallow it down. Swallowed anger tends to lodge in your favored part of the body and manifests itself through dis-ease. For years and years, you keep packing your anger into that same place.

So in order to heal, let your true feelings out. If you cannot express them to the person directly involved, go to a mirror and talk to that person. Express everything: "I'm angry at you." "I'm frightened." "I'm upset." "You hurt me." Just go on and on until all the anger is released. Then take a deep breath, look in the mirror, and ask: "What is the pattern that created this? What can I do to make a change?" If you can change the belief system inside that is creating this behavior, then you will not need to do it anymore.

One of the very worst things we can do

is to get angry at ourselves.

Anger only locks us more rigidly

into our patterns.

I AM FREE TO BE ME

Don't swallow your anger and have it settle in your body. When you get upset, give yourself a physical release. There are several methods you can use to release these feelings in positive ways. You can scream in the car with the windows closed. You can beat your bed or kick pillows. You can make noise and say all the things you want to say. You can scream into a pillow. You can run around a track, or play a game like tennis to release the energy. Beat the bed or kick pillows at least once a week, whether you feel angry or not . . . just to release those physical tensions you store in your body!

If we wait until we become perfect
before we love ourselves,
we will waste our lives.
We are already perfect
right here and right now.

I AM PERFECT EXACTLY AS I AM

You are neither too much nor too little. You do not have to prove to anyone or anything who you are. You are the perfect expression of the Oneness of Life. In the Infinity of Life you have been many identities, each one a perfect expression for that particular lifetime. Be content to be who and what you are in this life. Do not yearn to be like someone else, for that is not the expression you chose this time. Next time you will be different. You are perfect as you are, right here and right now. You are sufficient. You are one with all of Life.

There is no need to struggle to be better. All you need to do is to love yourself more today than yesterday and to treat yourself as someone who is deeply loved. Love is the nourishment that humans need to fulfill their greatness. As you learn to love yourself more, you learn to love *everyone* more.

Together we lovingly nourish an evermore beautiful world. We are all healed, and the planet is healed, too. With joy, we recognize our perfection and the perfection of Life. And so it is.

Life is very simple.

We create our experiences

by our thinking and feeling patterns.

What we believe about ourselves

and about Life becomes

true for us.

I CREATE Wonderful NEW BELIEFS FOR MYSELF

These are some of the beliefs that can really help you in your life if you think or say them every day:

I am always safe.

Everything I need to know is revealed to me.

Everything I need comes to me in the perfect time/space sequence.

Life is a joy and filled with love.

I prosper wherever I turn.

I am willing to change and to grow.

All is well in my world.

Notice what you are thinking at this moment.

Is the thought negative or positive?

Do you want this thought to be creating your

future and your infinite possibilities?

Just notice and be aware.

I EXPERIENCE THE TOTALITY OF POSSIBILITIES WITHIN ME

What does the totality of possibilities mean to you? Think of it as no limitations at all. Going beyond all limitations. Let your mind go beyond what you thought was possible: "It can't be done." "It won't work." "There's not enough." "This is in the way."

Think of how often you have expressed these limitations: "Because I'm a woman, I can't do this." "Because I'm a man, I can't do that." "I don't have the right education." You hold on to limitations because they are important to you. But limitations stop you from expressing and experiencing the totality of possibilities. Every time you say "I can't," you are limiting yourself. Are you willing to go beyond what you believe today?

If you work where there is love, joy,

and laughter, and you are appreciated,

you are going to do such a good job

and work twice as hard.

You will find that you have

more talents and abilities

than you ever knew you had.

OUR BUSINESS IS A DIVINE IDEA

Our business is a Divine idea in the One Mind, created out of Divine love and sustained by love. Every employee has been attracted by the action of love, for it is his or her Divine right place here at this point in time and space. Divine harmony permeates us all, and we flow together in a most productive and joyous way. It is the action of love that brought us to this particular place. Divine right action operates every aspect of our business. Divine Intelligence creates our products and services. Divine love brings to us those who can be helped by that which we so lovingly do.

We release all old patterns of complaining or condemning, for we know that it is our consciousness that creates our circumstances in the business world. We know and declare that it is possible to successfully operate our business according to Divine principles, and we lovingly use our mental tools to live and experience our lives more abundantly. We refuse to be limited in any way by human-mind thinking. The Divine Mind is our business consultant and has plans for us that we have not yet dreamed. Our lives are filled with love and joy because our business is a Divine idea. And so it is.

Rejoice in other
people's successes
because there is plenty
for everyone.

OUR BUSINESS IS PROSPEROUS

We are one with the Universal Mind, and therefore all wisdom and knowledge is available to us right here and right now. We are Divinely guided; and our business prospers, expands, and grows. We now choose to release any negative thoughts about cash-flow limitations. We open our consciousness to a quantum leap of prosperity by thinking and accepting that large amounts of money flood our bank account. We have plenty to use, to spare, and to share. The law of prosperity keeps the flow of cash moving in abundant amounts. It pays our bills and brings us everything we need.

Each of us within this organization prospers. We now choose to be living examples of prosperity consciousness. We live and work in comfort, ease, and beauty. We have inner peace and security. We watch with joy and gratitude as we and this business continually grow and prosper far beyond our expectations. We bless this business with love. And so it is.

You are continually successful

in each and every project you do.

All those with whom you do business

in any manner are also blessed

and prospered and are delighted

to be connected with you.

THIS BUSINESS IS GOD'S BUSINESS

We are in partnership with Divine Intelligence. We are not interested in the negative aspects of the outer business world, for they have nothing to do with us. We expect, and we receive, positive results. We attract to ourselves only those in the business world who operate on the highest level of integrity.

Everything we do is done in the most positive way. We are constantly grateful for the opportunities that are presented to us to help this planet and each person on it. We go within and connect with our higher intelligence, and we are always led and guided in ways that are for the highest benefit of all concerned. All of our equipment works perfectly. We are all healthy and happy. Everything is in harmony and flows in Divine right order. All is well. We know this to be true for us.

In order to change your life outside,

you must change inside.

The moment you are willing to change,

it is amazing how the Universe

begins to help you.

It brings you what you need.

ALL MY CHANGES ARE EASY TO MAKE

When we begin to work on ourselves, sometimes things get worse before they get better. It's okay if that happens. It's the beginning of the process. It's untangling old threads. We need to just flow with it. It takes time and effort to learn what we need to learn. We might not see changes instantly.

Impatience is only resistance to learning. It means we want the goal without going through the process. We need to let ourselves learn, step by step. It will get easier as we go along.

Say: "I am

willing to change."

Are you hesitating?

Do you feel that this is not true?

What is the belief that is in the way?

Remember: it is only a thought,

and a thought can be changed.

WHEN ONE DOOR CLOSES, ANOTHER DOOR OPENS

Life is a series of doors closing and opening. We walk from room to room having different experiences. Many of us would like to close some doors on old negative patterns, old blocks, and things that are no longer nourishing or useful for us. Many of us are in the process of opening new doors and finding wonderful new experiences—sometimes learning experiences and sometimes joyous experiences.

It is all part of Life, and we need to know that we really are safe. It is only change. From the very first door that we open when we come to this planet to the very last door that we open when we leave, we are always safe. It is only change. We are at peace with our own inner selves. We are safe and secure and loved.

Gentle, firm insistence and consistency

in what you choose to think

will make positive changes manifest

quickly and easily.

I AM WILLING TO CHANGE

Clasp your hands together. Which thumb is on top? Now unclasp them and clasp them together again with the *other* thumb on top. How does that feel? Different? Maybe it feels *wrong*. Unclasp your hands again and clasp them the other way, then the second way, then the first. How does it feel now? Not quite so *wrong?*

It's the same when you learn any new pattern. You need a little practice. You could do something the first time and say, "No, that's wrong," and never do it again, and you would go right back to being comfortable. If you're willing to practice a little bit, you'll find that you can be comfortable with the new thing. When you have something as important at stake as *you loving you,* it is well worth a little practice.

When we are ready to make

positive changes in our lives,

we attract whatever

we need to help us.

I AM WILLING TO CHANGE AND GROW

You are willing to learn new things because you do not know it all. You are willing to drop old concepts when they no longer work for you. You are willing to see situations about yourself and say, "I do not want to do that anymore." You know you can become more of who you are. Not a better person, because that implies that you are not good enough—but you can become *more* of who you are.

Growing and changing is exciting, even if you have to look at some painful things within yourself in order to do so.

What is important in this moment

is what you are choosing to think,

believe, and say right now.

These thoughts and words

will create your future.

Your thoughts form the experiences

of tomorrow, next week, next month,

and next year.

IT'S ONLY A THOUGHT, AND A THOUGHT CAN BE CHANGED

How many times have you refused to think a positive thought about yourself? Well, you can refuse to think negative thoughts about yourself, too. People say, "I can't stop thinking a thought." Yes, you can! You have to make up your mind that it's what you're going to do. You don't have to fight your thoughts when you want to change things. When that negative voice comes up, you can say, "Thank you for sharing, and I'm choosing to do something else. I don't want to buy into that anymore, I want to create another way of thinking."

Don't fight your thoughts. Acknowledge them and go beyond them.

Your parents were doing the best
they could do with the understanding
and awareness they had.
They could not teach you
anything they didn't know.
If your parents didn't love themselves,
there was no way they could
teach you to love yourself.

I CREATE A WONDERFUL FUTURE NOW

No matter what your early childhood was like—the best or the worst—you and only you are in charge of your life now. You can spend your time blaming your parents or your early environment, but all that accomplishes is keeping you stuck in victim patterns. It never gets you the good you say you want.

Your current thinking shapes your future. It can create a life of negativity and pain, or it can create a life of unlimited joy. Which one do you choose?

Children always do what *we* do.
You might examine what is keeping you
from loving yourself and be
willing to let this go.
You will be a wonderful example
to your children.

I COMMUNICATE OPENLY WITH MY CHILDREN

It is vitally important to keep the lines of communication open with children, especially during the teen years. Usually, when children start to talk about things, they are told over and over again: "Don't say this." "Don't do that." "Don't feel that." "Don't be that way." "Don't express that." "Don't, don't, don't!" So children cut themselves off. They stop communicating.

A few years later, when they grow older, parents start to say, "My children never call me." Why don't they call? Because the lines of communication have been cut off at some point.

Begin to listen to what you say

and how you say it.

Don't say anything that you

don't want to become true for you.

You can choose what to

say, do, and think.

EVERYTHING I DO IS BY CHOICE

Remove the expression *have to* from your vocabulary and your thinking, because it is going to release a lot of self-imposed pressure. You can create tremendous stress by saying: "I have to get up." "I have to do this." "I have to, I have to."

Instead, begin by saying, "I choose to." It puts a whole different perspective on your life. Everything you do is by choice. It may not seem so, but it is.

Know and affirm that you are

one with the Infinite Power,

and therefore your way is made

easy, smooth, and complete.

THIS DAY IS ONE OF COMPLETION

Each moment of your life is perfect, whole, and complete. With God, nothing is ever unfinished. You are one with Infinite Power, Infinite Wisdom, Infinite Action, and Infinite Oneness. You wake up with a sense of fulfillment, knowing that you shall complete all that you undertake today. Each breath is full and comes to completion. Each scene you see is complete in itself. Each word you speak is full and complete. Each task you undertake, or each portion of that task, is completed to your satisfaction. You do not struggle alone in the wilderness of life. You release all belief in struggle and resistance.

You accept assistance from your many unseen friends who are always ready to lead you and guide you as you allow them to help. Everything in your life falls into place easily and effortlessly. Calls are completed on time. Letters are received and answered. Projects come to fruition. Others cooperate. Everything is on time and in perfect Divine right order. All is complete, and you feel good. This is a day of completion. Declare that it is so.

Be aware that we are

all pure consciousness.

We are not lonely or lost or abandoned.

We are one with all of Life.

I AM PURE SPIRIT

Look within your very centered space and see the part of you that is pure spirit. Pure light. Pure energy. Visualize all your limitations falling away one by one, until you are safe, healed, and whole. Know that no matter what is going on in your life, no matter how difficult things may be, at the very center of your being you are safe and you are whole. You always will be.

Lifetime after lifetime, you are a shining spirit—a beautiful light. Sometimes you come to this planet and cover your light and hide it. But the light is always there. As you let those limitations go, and as you recognize the true beauty of your being, you shine brilliantly. You are love. You are energy. You are spirit. You are the spirit of love shining brightly. Let your light shine.

Every time you make

a judgment or criticism,

you are sending something out

that is going to

come back to you.

I LOVE BEING ME

Can you imagine how wonderful it would be if you could live your life without ever being criticized by anyone? Wouldn't it be wonderful to feel totally at ease, totally comfortable? You would get up in the morning and you would know you were going to have a wonderful day, because everybody would love you and nobody would put you down. You would just feel great.

You know what? You can give this to yourself. You can make the experience of living with *you* the most wonderful experience imaginable. You can wake up in the morning and feel the joy of spending another day with yourself.

Critical people often attract

a lot of criticism because

it is their *pattern* to criticize.

They often need to be perfect at all times.

Do you know *anyone* on this planet

who is perfect?

I LOVE AND ACCEPT MYSELF EXACTLY AS I AM

We all have areas of our lives that we think are unacceptable and unlovable. If we are really angry with parts of ourselves, we often engage in self-abuse. We abuse alcohol, drugs, or cigarettes; we overeat, or whatever. We beat ourselves up. One of the worst things we do, which does more damage than anything else, is criticize ourselves. We need to stop all criticism. Once we get into the practice of doing that, it is amazing how we stop criticizing other people—because everyone is a reflection of us, and what we see in another person we see in ourselves.

When we complain about another person, we are really complaining about ourselves. When we can truly love and accept who we are, there is nothing to complain about. We cannot hurt ourselves and we cannot hurt another person. Let's make a vow that we will no longer criticize ourselves for anything.

Some of the things you believe

were never true.

They were someone else's fears.

Give yourself a chance

to examine your thoughts.

Change those that are negative.

You are deserving.

I DESERVE GOOD IN MY LIFE

Sometimes when our inner messages are telling us that we are not allowed to be happy, or when we create good things in our lives and haven't changed those early messages, we will do something to thwart our happiness. When we don't believe that we deserve good, we will knock the supports out from under us. Sometimes we hurt ourselves, or develop physical problems, or have accidents.

We have to start believing that we deserve all the good that life has to offer.

We learn our belief systems
as very little children.
We then move through life
creating experiences
to match our beliefs.

I DESERVE JOY

Many of you believe that you deserve to live in an atmosphere of "not good enough." Start doing affirmations that reflect what you really deserve. State that you are willing to go beyond your parents' and your own early childhood limitations. Look in the mirror and say to yourself: "I deserve all good. I deserve to be prosperous. I deserve joy. I deserve love."

Open your arms wide and say: "I am open and receptive. I am wonderful. I deserve all good. I accept."

Wherever you go and whomever you meet,

you will find your own love,

and your highest good,

waiting for you.

I FOLLOW THE PATH OF RIGHT ACTION

In the Infinity of Life where you are, all is perfect, whole, and complete. Knowing that you are one with the Source and that you follow the path of right action, you are on principle at all times. You choose your thoughts to be in alignment with all that is for your highest good and greatest joy. Your quality of life reflects this state. You love life. You love yourself. You are safe at all times. All is well in your world.

A rose is always beautiful,

always perfect, and ever changing.

This is the way we are.

We are always perfect wherever

we are in life.

I AM IN THE RIGHT PLACE

Just as all the stars and planets are in their perfect orbit and in Divine right order, so are you. The heavens are in perfect alignment, and so are you. You may not understand everything that is going on with your limited human mind. However, you know that on the cosmic level, you must be in the right place, at the right time, doing the right thing. Positive thoughts are what you choose to think. This present experience is a stepping-stone to new awareness and greater glory.

Ask for help.

Tell Life what you want

and allow it to happen.

EVERYTHING I NEED COMES TO ME IN THE RIGHT TIME/SPACE SEQUENCE

Doing affirmations, making wish lists, creating treasure maps, doing visualizations, and writing in a journal can be compared to going to a restaurant. The waiter takes your order and then goes into the kitchen to give it to the chef. You sit there and do whatever you do, because you assume that the food is on its way. You don't ask the waiter every two seconds, "Is it ready yet? How are they making it? What are they doing in there?" You place your order and *know* that your food will be served to you.

It is much the same in the *cosmic kitchen* of the Universe. You place an order and know it is being taken care of. It will arrive in the perfect time/space sequence.

Find an image of something you really love:

flowers, a rainbow, a special song,

a beautiful place—whatever.

Let that be the image you envision

every time you start

to scare yourself.

I AM IN HARMONY WITH NATURE

This I know and affirm for myself: I love and approve of myself. All is well in my world. I inhale the precious yet abundant breath of Life and allow my body, mind, and emotions to relax. There is no need for me to scare myself. I am in harmony with all of Life— the sun, the moon, the winds, the rain, the earth, and the *movement* of the earth. The power that resettles the earth is my friend. I am at peace with the elements. Nature's elements are my friends. I am flexible and flowing. I am always safe and secure. I know that no harm can befall me.

I sleep and wake and move in complete safety. Not only am *I* safe, but my friends, family, and loved ones are safe as well. I trust in the power that created me to protect me at all times and under all circumstances. I create a reality for myself of oneness and security. Where I am, there is always an island of safety. I am safe; it's only change. I love and approve of myself. I trust myself. All is well in my world.

Release the emotional attachment

to beliefs from the past

so that they don't hurt you in the present.

If you live fully in the moment,

you cannot be hurt by the past,

no matter what it was.

I AM always SAFE

When you hold your emotions down or hold things in, you create havoc within you. Love yourself enough to allow yourself to *feel* your emotions. Addictions such as alcohol mask the emotions so that you don't feel. Allow your feelings to come to the surface. You may have to process quite a bit of old "stuff." Start doing some affirmations for yourself so that you can do this easily, smoothly, and comfortably. Affirm that you are willing to feel your true emotions and, most important, keep telling yourself that you are safe.

There are people looking

for the exact skills and talents

you have to offer,

and you are being brought together

on the checkerboard of Life.

I REJOICE IN MY EMPLOYMENT

I affirm the following: My job is to express God. I rejoice in this employment. I give thanks for every opportunity to demonstrate the power of Divine Intelligence to work through me. Anytime I am presented with a challenge, I know that it is an opportunity from God, my employer; and I quiet my intellect, turn within, and wait for positive words to fill my mind. I accept these blessed revelations with joy and know that I am worthy of my just reward for a job well done.

In exchange for this exhilarating position, I am abundantly compensated. My fellow employees—all of humankind—are supportive, loving, cheerful, enthusiastic, and powerful workers in the field of spiritual unfoldment, whether they choose to be aware of it or not. I see them as perfect expressions of the One Mind diligently applying themselves to their jobs. Working for this unseen yet ever-present Chief Operating Officer, the Ultimate Chairman of the Board, I know that my creative activity elicits financial abundance, for the job of expressing God is ever rewarded.

Feel that bounce in your step.

See your shining eyes.

The radiant you is right here.

Claim it!

I AM HEALTHY AND FILLED WITH ENERGY

You know and affirm that your body is a friendly place to live. You have respect for your body and treat it well. You connect with the energy of the Universe and allow it to flow through you.

You have wonderful energy that sustains you throughout each day. You are radiant, vital, and alive. And so it is!

Today is a very exciting time of your life.

You are on a wonderful adventure

and will never go through

this particular process again.

I AM ON AN EVER-CHANGING JOURNEY

In the Infinity of Life, all is perfect, whole, and complete. The cycle of Life is also perfect, whole, and complete. There is a time of beginning, a time of growth, a time of being, a time of withering or wearing out, and a time of leaving. These are all part of the perfection of Life. We sense it as normal and natural, and though saddened at times, we accept the cycle and its rhythms.

Sometimes there is a sudden abrupt ending midcycle. We are jarred and feel threatened. Someone died too young or something was smashed and broken. Often thoughts that create pain remind us of our mortality—we, too, have an ending to our cycle. Shall we live out its fullness, or will we also have an early ending? Life is ever changing. There is no beginning and no end, only a constant cycling and recycling of substance and experience. Life is never stuck or static or stale, for each moment is ever new and fresh. Every ending is a new point of beginning.

We are on an endless journey

through eternity.

We have lifetime after lifetime.

What we don't work out in one life,

we will work out in another.

THERE IS NO DEATH

Our spirit can never be taken from us, for it is the part of us that is eternal. No argument can take it from us. No loss of relationship can take it from us. No death can take it from us. Our spirit is the part of us that goes on forever. All the people we know who have left the planet are still here in pure essence and pure spirit. They always have been, they are now, and they always will be. It is true that we will not connect with their physical bodies again, but when we leave our bodies, our spirits will connect. There is no loss. There is no death. There is only a cycling and recycling of energies—a changing of form.

When we connect with our spirits, we go beyond all petty things. Our understanding is so great. Our spirit, our soul—the very essence of who we are—is always safe, secure, and alive. And so it is.

By practicing breathing,

you drop the barriers

holding you back

and begin to open up and expand.

It is a beginning point.

I BREATHE IN LOVE AND FLOW WITH LIFE

Are you expanding or contracting? When you expand your thinking, your beliefs, and everything about yourself, the love flows freely. When you contract, you put up walls and shut yourself off. If you are frightened or threatened or feeling that something is not right, begin to breathe. Breathing opens you up. It straightens your spine. It opens your chest. It gives your heart room to expand.

Instead of going into total panic, take a few breaths and ask yourself, "Do I want to contract or do I want to expand?"

This is a new day.

Begin anew to claim and create

all that is good.

I EXPRESS MY
TRUE BEING

I affirm the following: I see myself having a consciousness of oneness with the presence and power of God. I see myself ever aware of the power of God within me as the source of everything I desire. I see myself confidently calling upon the Presence to supply my every need. I love all expressions of God unconditionally, knowing the truth of all that is. I walk through life with the happy companionship of my Godself, and joyfully express the goodness that I am. My wisdom and understanding of Spirit increases, and I express more fully each day the inner beauty and strength of my true being.

Divine order is ever present in my experience, and there is plenty of time for all that I choose to do. I express wisdom, understanding, and love in all my dealings with others; and my words are Divinely guided. I see myself expressing the creative energy of Spirit in my work, writing and speaking words of truth easily and with a depth of understanding and wisdom. Fun, uplifting ideas flow through my consciousness for joyful expression, and I follow through on the ideas received, bringing them into full manifestation.

It is your birthright

to express yourself

in ways that are

fulfilling to you.

I FREELY EXPRESS WHO I AM

You are indeed blessed. There are wonderful opportunities to be yourself, to express yourself as who you really are. You are the beauty and joy of the Universe expressing and receiving. You surround yourself with Divine honesty and justice. You know that Divine right action is taking place, and whatever the outcome, it is perfect for you and everyone concerned.

You are one with the very Power that created you. You are wonderful. You rejoice in the truth of your being. You accept it as so and let it be. You say, "So be it," and know that all is well in your wonderful world right here and right now.

If you *want* love and acceptance
from your family, then you must
give love and acceptance
to them.

I BLESS MY FAMILY WITH LOVE

This I know to be true: Not everyone has the special family that I have, nor do they have the opportunities to open their hearts in the way my family does. We are not limited by what the neighbors think or by society's prejudices. We are far more than that. We are a family that comes from love, and we accept with pride every unique member.

I am special, and worthy of love. I love and accept each member of my wonderful family; and they, in turn, love and adore me. I am safe. All is well in my world.

How are you treating

your parents or grandparents?

What you give out is

what you are

going to get when

you grow older.

I HAVE LOVING COMPASSION FOR MY FATHER

If you have any "stuff" with your father, do a meditation in your mind and talk with him so that you can clean up any old issues. Forgive him or forgive yourself. Tell him that you love him just as he is.

Get cleaned up in your mind so that you can move into feeling more deserving of all that is good.

Sometimes when your life is magnificent,

you may fear that something bad

is going to happen to take it all away.

Anxiety is fear, and not trusting yourself.

Just recognize it as the part of you

that is used to being upset about something,

thank it for sharing, and then let it go.

I AM *always* PERFECTLY PROTECTED

Remember, when a fearful thought comes up, it is trying to protect you. Isn't that what fear is all about? When you become frightened, your adrenaline pumps up to protect you from danger.

Say to the fear: "I appreciate that you want to help me." Then, do an affirmation about that particular fear. Acknowledge and thank the fear, but don't give it importance.

We do not have to know

how to forgive.

All we have to do

is be willing to forgive.

The Universe will take care

of the how.

I FORGIVE ALL PAST EXPERIENCES

When the word *forgiveness* is mentioned, who comes to your mind? Who is the person or what is the experience that you feel you will never forget, never forgive? What is it that holds you to the past? When you refuse to forgive, you hold on to the past, and it is impossible for you to be in the present. It is only when you are in the present that you can create your future. Forgiving is a gift to yourself. It frees you from the past, the past experience, and past relationships. It allows you to live in present time. When you forgive yourself and forgive others, you are indeed free.

There is a tremendous sense of freedom that comes with forgiveness. Often you need to forgive yourself for putting up with painful experiences and not loving yourself enough to move away from those experiences. So love yourself, forgive yourself, forgive others, and be in the moment. See the old bitterness and the old pain just roll off your shoulders as you let the doors of your heart open wide. When you come from a space of love, you are always safe. Forgive everyone. Forgive yourself. Forgive all past experiences. You are free.

You can choose to be that part

of your spirit that is totally free.

If you can be free in one area,

you can be free in many areas.

Be willing to be free.

I AM FREE

I affirm the following: I am pure spirit and light and energy. I see myself as being free. I am free in my mind. I am free in my emotions. I am free in my relationships. I am free in my body. I am free in my life. I allow myself to connect to that part of me that is pure spirit and that is totally free. I release all of my limitations and my human-mind fears. I no longer feel stuck.

I realize that I am far more than my personality, my problems, or my dis-ease. The more I connect with this part of me, the more I can be free in every area of my life. The part of me that is pure spirit knows how to lead me and guide me in ways that are very beneficial. I trust the spirit part of me, and know that it is safe for me to be free. I am free in my love for myself. I let that love for myself flow as freely as possible. It is safe to be free. I am spirit, and I am free.

Be good to yourself

by enjoying yourself every day in every way.

Feel free to let loose and have fun.

I CAN CREATE FUN IN MY LIFE

You are grown up now! You can do anything you want to do. Whenever you do what pleases you, wonderful things occur. It is a way of being nurturing to yourself, and as you do so, you find more fun in your world. You are *allowed* to have more fun. The more fun you have, the more other people love you.

You love and approve of who you are, and you feel good about yourself. All is well in your fun-filled world.

A tragedy can turn out

to be our greatest gift if we approach it

in a positive and nurturing way.

I LET THE LIGHT OF MY LO♥VE SHINE

When we are in pain or afraid or grieving and we see a light in the darkness, we don't feel so alone. Let's think of this light as someone's love shining upon us. It gives us warmth and comfort. Each of us has the light of our love within us. We can let our light shine so it will nurture us and be a great comfort to others.

We all know people who have passed on. See their light shining, and let their love surround us and soothe us. Each one of us has an infinite supply of love to give. The more we give, the more there is to give. Yes, sometimes it hurts to feel, but thank God we *can* feel. Let us be comforted and be at peace. And so it is.

We can grow up to be the joyous,

unlimited beings we always knew

we could be.

I TREAT
MYSELF WITH
unconditional
LOVE

If your childhood was full of fear and fighting, and you mentally beat yourself up now, you are continuing to treat your inner child much the same. The child has no place to go within you. Love yourself enough now to go beyond your parents' limitations. They did not know any other way to train you.

You have been a good little child for a long time, doing exactly what Mommy and Daddy taught you. It is time for you to grow up and make adult decisions that support and nourish you.

Guilt never makes anyone feel better,

nor does it change a situation.

Stop feeling guilty.

Let yourself out of jail.

I FORGIVE MYSELF FOR ANY wrongdoing

So many of you live under a heavy cloud of guilt. You always feel wrong. You are not doing it right. You are apologizing all the time. You will not forgive yourself for something you did in the past. You manipulate others as you once were manipulated. Guilt does not solve anything. If you really did something in the past that you are sorry about, stop doing it! If you can make amends to the other party, do it. If not, then don't do it again.

Guilt looks for punishment, and punishment creates pain. Forgive yourself and forgive others. Step out of your self-imposed prison.

Everything in your life—

every experience, every relationship—

is a mirror of the mental pattern

that is going on inside of you.

When these patterns change for the better,

you create harmony within.

I AM A harmonious BEING

I affirm the following: I am at the heart of the Divine Mind—perfect, whole, and complete. All my affairs are Divinely guided into right action with perfect results. Everything I do, say, or think is in harmony with truth. There is perfect and continuous right action in my life and in my affairs. It is safe for me to change. I release all thoughts or vibrations of confusion, chaos, dis-harmony, dis-respect, or dis-trust. These thoughts are eliminated from my consciousness completely.

I am harmoniously linked with everyone I am in contact with. People love working and being with me. I express my thoughts, feelings, and ideas; and they are easily welcomed and comprehended by others. I am a loving, joyful person, and everybody loves me. I am safe. I am welcomed with joy wherever I am. All is well in my world, and life gets better all the time.

Search your heart for feelings

of injustice and unfairness

that you feel have been inflicted upon you

at work, and let them go.

You are free.

I AM CENTERED iN truth AND PEACE

I affirm the following: No matter where I am, there is only Spirit, God, Infinite good, Infinite wisdom, Infinite harmony, and love. It cannot be otherwise. There is no duality. Therefore, right here and right now in my workplace, I declare and affirm that there is only Infinite harmony, wisdom, and love. There are no problems that do not have solutions. There are no questions without answers. I now choose to go beyond the problem to seek the Divine right action solution to any discord that may seem to appear in the true harmonious atmosphere of this business. I am willing to learn and grow from this seeming discord and confusion. I release all blame and turn within to seek the truth. I am also willing to release whatever pattern in our consciousness that has contributed to this situation.

I choose to know the truth, and the truth sets me free. Divine wisdom, Divine harmony, and Divine love reign supreme within me and around me and around each and every person in this office. This business is God's business; and God is now directing, leading, and guiding all of our movements. I declare for myself and for each and every person in this business peace, security, harmony, and a deep sense of love for the self and the joyous willingness to love others. We are all centered in truth and live in joy.

Healing means accepting
all parts of ourselves,
not just the parts we like,
but all of us.

I HEAL MYSELF ON ALL LEVELS

This is a time of compassion and a time of healing. Go within and connect with that part of yourself that knows how to heal. It is possible. Know that you are in the process of healing. Discover your healing abilities—those that are strong and powerful. You are incredibly capable. Be willing to go to a new level to find abilities and capabilities that you were not aware of so you can truly heal yourself on all possible levels.

You are spirit, and being spirit, you are free to save yourself . . . and the world. And so it is.

Dis-ease often breeds
in feelings of unforgiveness.
Forgiving others and
releasing resentment can help
create an atmosphere of healing,
and even dissolve dis-eases
such as cancer.

I AM A MAGNET FOR MIRACLES

Unknown and unexpected good is coming my way this day. I am far more than rules and regulations—restrictions and limitations. I change my consciousness, forgive those I need to forgive, and healing miracles occur.

Within every medical establishment there are practitioners who are enlightened and on a spiritual pathway. I now attract these people to me wherever I am. My mental atmosphere of love, acceptance, and forgiveness is a magnet for small miracles every moment of the day. Wherever I am, there is a healing atmosphere, and it blesses and brings peace to me and to all those around me.

If we don't make internal changes,

the dis-ease either comes back

or we create another dis-ease.

We can learn to heal ourselves.

I LET MY whole BEING VIBRATE WITH LIGHT

Look deep within the center of your heart and find that tiny pinpoint of brilliantly colored light. It is such a beautiful color. It is the very center of your love and healing energy. Watch as your pinpoint of light begins to pulsate and grow until it fills your heart. Let it move through your body from the top of your head to the tips of your toes. You are absolutely glowing with this beautifully colored light, which is your love and your healing energy. Let your body vibrate with this light.

You can even say to yourself: "With every breath I take, I'm getting healthier and healthier." Feel the light cleansing your body of dis-ease. Let the light radiate from you into your room, into the world, and into your special place in the world. See everything whole. You are important. You do count. What you do with the love in your heart does matter. You do make a difference. And so it is.

Every illness holds a lesson

for us to learn.

When we take this lesson

to heart,

our lives improve

as a result.

MY HANDS ARE POWERFUL HEALING TOOLS

The laying on of hands is normal and natural. It is a very ancient process. You know that if your body hurts, the first thing you do is place your hand over the spot to make it feel better. So allow yourself to give energy to yourself. Take a deep breath and release tension or fear or anger or pain, and let the love flow from your heart. Let your heart open so you can receive the love coming into your body. Your body knows exactly what to do with this healing energy and how to use it. See the light of love coming from your heart—a beautiful, wondrous light. Let that love come rolling from your heart, through your arms, and into your hands. That light penetrates your very being with compassion, understanding, and caring.

See yourself as whole and healed. Your hands are powerful. You deserve love. You deserve to be at peace. You deserve to feel safe. You deserve to be cared for. Allow yourself to receive.

We can choose

to surround ourselves

with healing, nurturing people

who support our

health and well-being.

EVERY HAND THAT TOUCHES ME IS A HEALING HAND

I affirm the following: I am a precious being and loved by the Universe. As I increase the love I have for myself, so too does the Universe mirror this, increasing love evermore abundantly. I know that the Universal Power is everywhere—in every person, place, and thing. This loving, healing power flows through the medical profession and is in every hand that touches my body.

I attract only highly evolved individuals on my healing pathway. My presence helps to bring out the spiritual, healing qualities in each practitioner. Doctors and nurses are amazed at their abilities to work as a healing team with me.

The body, like everything else in life,

is a mirror of your

inner thoughts and beliefs.

Every cell responds to

every single thought you think

and every word you speak.

I LISTEN CAREFULLY TO MY BODY'S MESSAGES

In this world of change, you choose to be flexible in all areas. You are willing to change yourself and your beliefs to improve the quality of your life and your world. Your body loves you in spite of how you may treat it. Your body communicates with you, and you now listen to its messages. You are willing to *get* the message. You pay attention and make the necessary corrections. You give your body what it needs on every level to bring it back to optimal health. You call upon an inner strength that is yours whenever you need it. And so it is.

Good health is having no fatigue;

having a good appetite;

going to sleep and awakening easily;

having a good memory;

having good humor;

having precision in thought and action;

and being honest, humble, grateful, and loving.

How healthy are you?

MY MIND, BODY, AND SPIRIT ARE A HEALTHY TEAM

The body is always talking to you. What do you do when you get a message from your body, such as a little ache or pain? Usually, you run to the medicine cabinet or the drugstore and take a pill. In effect you say to the body, "Shut up! I don't want to hear you. Don't talk to me!" That is not loving the body. When you get the first ache or pain or the slightest thing seems to go wrong, sit down, close your eyes, and very quietly ask yourself, "What is it I need to know?" Listen a few minutes for the answer. It may be as simple as "Get some sleep." Or it may be stronger.

If you want your body to work well for you for the long term, then you need to be part of the body, mind, and spirit healing team.

This is a time of the year

when we need to let

the spirit of love

flow through us.

We are on this planet to

surround ourselves

and others

with love.

LET THE SPIRIT OF LOVE FLOW THROUGH YOU

Go back in time and remember the very best holiday season you had as a child. Bring the memory up in your mind and see it very clearly. Remember the sights, the smells, the tastes, the touches, and the people who were there. What were some of the things you did? If you never had a wonderful holiday season as a child, then make one up. Picture it exactly as you would like it to be. As you think of this special time, notice that your heart is opening. Perhaps one of the most wonderful things about that particular season was the love that was present. Let the spirit of love flow through you now. Bring into your heart all the people you know and care about. Surround them with this love.

Know that you can carry this special feeling of the holidays with you everywhere and have it all the time, not just during one season of the year. You are love. You are spirit. You are light. You are energy. And so it is.

If you want to move from where you are,

thank your present home for being there for you.

Appreciate it. Don't say,

"Oh, I hate this place," because then you

aren't going to find something you really love.

Love where you are so you can open

yourself to a wonderful new place.

MY HOME IS A PEACEFUL HAVEN

Look at your home. Is it a place where you really want to live? Is it comfortable and joyous, or is it cramped and dirty and always messy? If you don't feel good about it, you are never going to enjoy it. Your home is a reflection of you. What state is it in? Clean out your closets and refrigerator. Take all the stuff in the closets that you haven't worn in a period of time and sell it, give it away, or burn it. Get rid of it so that you can make room for the new. As you let it go, say: "I'm cleaning out the closets of my mind." Do the same with your refrigerator. Clean out all the foods and scraps that have been there for a while.

People who have very cluttered closets and cluttered refrigerators have cluttered minds. Make your home a wonderful place to live in.

Money is energy;

it is an exchange of services.

It is matter and form.

It has no meaning in and of itself

except what we give it and believe about it.

We have so much "stuff" about money,

but it really is about what

we believe we deserve.

MY INCOME IS CONSTANTLY INCREASING

The quickest way to increase your income is to do the mental work. What can you do to help yourself? You can either choose to attract or repel money and other forms of prosperity. Complaining never works. You have a cosmic mental bank account, and you can deposit positive affirmations and believe you deserve—or not.

Affirm: "My income is constantly increasing. I am worthy of prosperity and abundance."

You can spend your time

griping and begrudging the things that

went wrong or how you are not good enough,

or you can spend your time

thinking about joyous experiences.

Loving yourself and thinking joyful,

happy thoughts is the quickest route

you can take to create

a wonderful life.

I HAVE UNLIMITED POTENTIAL

In the Infinity of Life where we all are, all is perfect, whole, and complete. We rejoice in knowing we are one with the Power that created us. This Power loves all its creations, including us. We are the beloved children of the Universe and have been given everything. We are the highest form of life on this planet and have been equipped with all that we need for every experience we shall have. Our minds are always connected to the One Infinite Mind; therefore, all knowledge and wisdom is available to us if we believe it is so.

We trust ourselves to create only that which is for our highest good and greatest joy—that which is perfect for our spiritual growth and evolution. We love who we are. We are particularly delighted with the incarnation we have chosen this lifetime. We know that we can, from moment to moment, shape and reshape our personalities and even our bodies to further express our greatest potential. We rejoice in our unlimitedness and know that before us lies the totality of possibilities in every area. We trust totally in the One Power, and we know that all is well in our world.

Be gentle, kind, and comforting
with your inner child as you
uncover and release the old,
negative messages within you.
Say: "All my changes are
comfortable, easy, and fun."

I LOVE MYSELF TOTALLY IN THE NOW

Love is the biggest eraser there is. Love erases even the deepest imprinting, because love goes deeper than anything. If your childhood imprinting was very strong and you keep saying, "It's all their fault; I can't change," you stay stuck.

Do a lot of mirror work. Love yourself in the mirror from the top of your head to the tips of your toes—both clothed and naked. Look into your eyes and love yourself and the child within.

Each one of us is always working

with the three-year-old child within us.

Most of us, unfortunately, spend

our time yelling at that child

and then wondering why

our lives don't work.

I EMBRACE MY INNER CHILD WITH LOVE

Take care of your inner child. It is the child who is frightened. It is the child who is hurting. It is the child who does not know what to do. Be there for your child. Embrace it and love it and do whatever you can to take care of its needs. Be sure to let your child know that no matter what happens, you will always be there for it. You will never turn away or desert it. You will always love this child.

You cannot learn other
people's lessons for them.
They must do the work themselves,
and they will do it when they are ready.

I LEARN SOMETHING NEW EVERY DAY

Wouldn't it be wonderful if, instead of having to memorize all those battle dates, children were taught how to think, how to love themselves, how to have good relationships, how to be wise parents, how to handle money, and how to be healthy? Very few of us have been taught how to handle these different areas of our lives. If we knew, we would do it differently.

If you have a habit or
pattern you'd like to change,
ask yourself how it serves you.
What do you get out of it?
If you no longer had it,
what would happen?
Very often, people say,
"My life would be better."
Why do you believe that you don't
deserve to have a better life?

I LET GO OF THE NEED FOR THIS CONDITION IN MY LIFE

We create habits and patterns because they serve us in some way. Sometimes we're punishing someone or loving someone. It is amazing how many illnesses we create because we want to punish a parent or love a parent. For example, "I'm going to have diabetes just like my daddy, because I love my daddy." It may not always be on a conscious level, but when we start looking within, we find the pattern. We often create negativity because we do not know how to handle some area of our lives. We need to ask ourselves: "What am I feeling sorry about?" "Who am I angry at?" "What am I trying to avoid?" "How will this save me?"

If we are not ready to let something go—really wanting to hold on to it because it serves us—it doesn't matter what we do; it will not work. When we are ready to let it go, it is amazing how the smallest thing can help us release it.

You not only have individual beliefs,

you also have family and societal beliefs.

Ideas are contagious.

I AM GOOD ENOUGH

If there is any belief within you that says you "can't have" or you're "not good enough," say to yourself: "I am willing to let that belief go. I do not have to believe that anymore." Please do not struggle. It is not hard work. You are just changing a thought. You were born to enjoy life. Affirm that you are now willing to open yourself up to the abundance and prosperity that is available everywhere. Claim your birthright here and right now: "I deserve to be prosperous. I deserve my good."

That which you have declared is already accomplished in consciousness, and now becomes manifest in your experience.

If you have been a very negative person
who criticizes yourself and everyone else
and sees life through very negative
and limiting eyes, then it's going to
take time for you to start
turning around and become loving.
You need to be patient with yourself.
Don't get angry with yourself because
you're not doing it fast enough.

I DECLARE
RICHNESS AND
FULLNESS
FOR MY LIFE

I affirm the following: I now choose to move away from the limiting beliefs that have been denying me the benefits I so desire. I declare that every negative thought pattern in my consciousness is now being cleared out, erased, and let go. My consciousness is now being filled with cheerful, positive, loving thought patterns that contribute to my health, wealth, and loving relationships. I now release all negative patterns that have contributed to fear of loss, fear of the dark, fear of being harmed, or fear of poverty. I also release those that have brought me pain, loneliness, self-abuse, undeservingness, burdens or losses of any sort, and any other nonsense that may be lingering in some dark corner of my consciousness.

I am now free to allow the good to manifest in my life. I declare for myself the richness and fullness of life in all its profuse abundance: love—lavishly flowing; prosperity—abounding; health—vital and vibrant; creativity—ever new and fresh; and peace—all-surrounding.

All this I deserve and am now willing to accept and have on a permanent basis. I am a co-creator with the One Infinite Allness of Life, and the totality of possibilities lies before me.

You are never lost,

as you are a part

of the Divine Mind,

where nothing is ever lost.

I TRUST THE INTELLiGENCE WITHIN ME

There is One Intelligence. It is everywhere, equally present. This Intelligence is within you and is in everything that you're looking for. When you get lost or lose something, don't start going into "I am in the wrong place; I won't find my way." Stop it. Know that the Intelligence within you and the Intelligence in what you are looking for now brings you together.

Nothing is ever lost in the Divine Mind. Trust this Intelligence within you.

One of the bonuses of
loving yourself and loving others
is that it makes you
feel so good.

MY LOVE IS LIMITLESS

We have so much love in this world and so much love in our hearts, but sometimes we forget. Sometimes we think there isn't enough or there is just a small amount. So we hoard what we have or we are afraid to let it go. We are afraid to let it out. But those of us who are willing to learn realize that the more love we allow to flow out from us, the more there is within us . . . and the more we receive. It is endless and timeless.

Love is really the most powerful healing force there is. Without love, we could not survive at all. If tiny babies are not given love and affection, they wither and die. Most of us think we can survive without love, but we cannot. Love for ourselves is the power that heals us. So we need to be as loving as we can, every day.

At least three times a day,

stand with your arms open wide and say:

"I am willing to let the love in.

It is safe to let the love in."

I AM WORTH LOVING

You don't have to earn love any more than you have to earn the right to breathe. You have a right to breathe . . . because you exist. You have a right to be loved . . . because you exist. That is all you need to know. You are worthy of your own love. Don't allow society's negative opinions, or your parents or friends, make you think that you are not good enough. The reality of your being is that you are lovable. Accept this and know this. When you really do, you will find that people treat you as a lovable person.

Every time you meditate,

do a visualization for healing,

or say something geared

toward healing the entire planet,

you are connecting with like-minded people

all over the world.

I HELP CREATE A WORLD WHERE WE ARE SAFE TO LOVE EACH OTHER

We can help create a world where it is safe for us to love each other—where we can be loved and accepted exactly as we are. It is something we all wanted when we were children—to be loved and accepted exactly as we were. Not when we got taller or brighter or prettier, or more like our cousin or sister or neighbor across the way. But to be loved and accepted exactly as we were.

We grow up and want the same—to be loved and accepted exactly as we are right here and right now. But we are not going to get it from other people unless we can give it to ourselves first. When we can love ourselves, it becomes easier for us to love other people. When we love ourselves, we don't hurt ourselves and we don't hurt other people. We let go of all prejudices and beliefs about one group or another not being good enough. When we realize how incredibly beautiful we all are, we have the answer to world peace—a world where it is safe for us to love each other.

If you believe
you did something wrong,
then you are going to find
a way to punish yourself.

I RISE ABOVE ALL LIMITATIONS

Each experience is a stepping-stone in life, including any so-called mistakes. Love yourself for all your mistakes. They have been very valuable to you. They have taught you many things. It is the way you learn. Be willing to stop punishing yourself for your mistakes. Love yourself for your willingness to learn and grow.

Respect your parents for who they are—
not for whom you wish they would be.
Give love unconditionally,
and speak up for what you want.
Your relationship will get better.

I HAVE A RELATIONSHIP WITH MY MOTHER, THAT SERVES US BOTH

What kind of relationship would you like to have with your mother? Put it into affirmative treatment form, and start declaring it for yourself. Then you can tell her. If she is still pushing your buttons, you are not letting her know how you feel. You have a right to have the life you want. You have a right to be an adult. It may not be easy. Decide what it is you need. She may not approve of it, but don't make her wrong. Tell her what you need.

Ask her: "How can we work this out?"
Say to her: "I want to love you, and I want to have a wonderful relationship with you, but I need to be myself."

A thought such as *I am a bad person*

produces a negative feeling.

However, if you do not

have such a thought,

you will not have that feeling.

Change the thought,

and the feeling will go.

I AM NOW WILLING TO SEE ONLY MY MAGNIFICENCE

Choose to eliminate from your mind and life every negative, destructive, fearful idea and thought. No longer listen to or become part of detrimental thoughts or conversations. Today, no one can harm you because you refuse to believe in being hurt. No matter how justified it may seem to be, you refuse to indulge in damaging emotions. You rise above anything that attempts to make you angry or afraid. Destructive thoughts have no power over you.

Guilt does not change the past. You think and say only what you want to create in your life. You are more than adequate for all you need to do. You are one with the power that created you. You are safe. All is well in your world.

Make this your new motto:

"I go for the joy!

Life is here for me

to enjoy today!"

THIS YEAR I DO THE MENTAL WORK for CHANGE

Many of you start New Year's resolutions on the first of the year, but because you don't make internal changes, the resolutions fall away very quickly. Until you make the inner changes and are willing to do some mental work, nothing *out there* is going to change. The only thing you need to change is a thought—only a thought. Even self-hatred is only hating a thought you have about yourself.

What can you do for yourself this year in a positive way? What would you like to do this year that you did not do last year? What would you like to let go of this year that you clung to so tightly last year? What would you like to change in your life? Are you willing to do the work that will bring about those changes?

Observe what is going on
in your life and know that you are
not your experiences.

I NOTICE WHAT IS GOING ON INSIDE OF ME

What do you need to do to get to that space where you could be the happiest and most powerful person in your world? If you have done a lot of work on yourself, and you understand the principle that what you think and say goes out from you, and the Universe responds and it comes back, then observe yourself. Watch yourself without judgment and without criticism. This seems to be one of the biggest hurdles you have to overcome. Just look at yourself objectively—all the things about you. Just note what they are without making comments. Just observe.

As you allow yourself the space to go inside and begin to notice what is going on—how you feel, how you react, what you believe—you come from a space where you are much more open.

We can either destroy the planet

or we can heal it.

It is up to us individually.

We need to sit down every day and send

some loving, healing energy to the planet.

What we do with our minds

makes a difference.

I AM CONNECTED TO ALL LIFE

I affirm the following: I am spirit, light, energy, vibration, color, and love. I am so much more than I give myself credit for. I am connected with every person on the planet and with all of Life. I see myself healthy, whole, and living in a society where it is safe for me to be who I am and for all of us to love one another.

I hold this vision for myself and for all of us, for it is a time of healing and making whole. I am part of that whole. I am one with all Life. And so it is.

Our spiritual growth

often comes to us in ways

that we don't quite expect.

I OPEN NEW DOORS TO LIFE

You are standing in the corridor of Life, and behind you so many doors have closed. Things you no longer do or say or think. Experiences you no longer have. Ahead of you is an unending corridor of doors—each one opening to a new experience. As you move forward, see yourself opening various doors on wonderful experiences that you would like to have. Trust that your inner guide is leading you and guiding you in ways that are best for you, and that your spiritual growth is continuously expanding. No matter which door opens or which door closes, you are always safe. You are eternal. You will go on forever from experience to experience.

See yourself opening doors to joy, peace, healing, prosperity, and love. Doors to understanding, compassion, and forgiveness. Doors to freedom. Doors to self-worth and self-esteem. Doors to self-love. It is all here before you. Which door will you open first? Remember, you are safe; it is only change.

Fear comes from not trusting

the process of Life to be there for you.

The next time you are frightened, say:

"I trust the process of Life

to take care of me."

ALL MY EXPERIENCES ARE RIGHT FOR ME

We have been going through doors since the moment we were born. That was a big door and a big change. We came to this planet to experience Life this particular time around. We chose our parents, and we have been through many doors since then. We came equipped with everything within us that we need in order to live this Life fully and richly. We have all the wisdom. We have all the knowledge. We have all the abilities and all the talents. We have all the love and all the emotions that we need. Life is here to support us and take care of us, and we need to know and trust that it is so. Doors are constantly closing and constantly opening, and if we stay centered in ourselves, then we are always safe no matter which doorway we pass through.

Even when we pass through the last doorway on this planet, it is not the end. It is the beginning of another new adventure. It is all right to experience change. Today is a new day. We will have many wonderful new experiences. We are loved. We are safe. And so it is.

Don't run around and try

to heal all of your friends.

Do your own mental work

and heal yourself.

This will do more good for those

around you than anything else.

I ALLOW OTHERS TO BE THEMSELVES

We cannot force others to change. We can offer them a positive mental atmosphere where they have the possibility to change if they wish. But we cannot do it for, or to, other people. Everyone is here to work out their own lessons, and if we fix it for them, then they will just go and do it again, because they have not worked out what they needed to do for themselves. All we can do is love them. Allow them to be who they are. Know that the truth is always within them and that they can change at any moment they want.

If we have a compulsive habit in any area,

instead of thinking how terrible we are,

let us realize that there is some need

in our consciousness to

have this condition

or it would not be there.

I AM SAFE AND SECURE IN MY WORLD

Overweight has always meant protection. When you feel insecure or frightened, you pad yourself with protection. Most of you spend your time being angry at yourselves for being fat and have guilt over food. Weight has nothing to do with the food. There is something going on in your life that is making you feel insecure. You can fight fat for 20 years and still be fat because you have not dealt with the cause. If you are overweight, put the weight issue aside and work on the other issue first—the pattern that says: "I need protection" and "I'm insecure." Don't get angry when the weight goes on, because our cells respond to our mental patterns. When the need for the protection is gone or when we start feeling secure, the fat will melt off by itself.

Begin to say: "I used to have a problem with weight." You will begin to shift the pattern. What you choose to think today will start creating your new figure tomorrow.

People who are addicted

are usually running from themselves,

and they use some sort of addiction

to fill the space inside.

I AM WILLING TO RELEASE MY FEARS

If you are overweight, you can have all the willpower and discipline in the world and go on all sorts of diets. You can be really strong, and for months you may not eat one mouthful of food that you *shouldn't* eat. Unfortunately, the moment you drop your willpower and discipline, the weight comes back again. It is because you have not dealt with the real issue. You have only worked on the outer effect. The real issue with weight is usually fear, which creates fat for protection. You can fight fat all your life and never get to the real issue. You could probably die believing that you were not good enough because you could not lose the weight.

However, if your need to feel safe could be fulfilled in a more positive way, then the weight would leave by itself. Say: "I am willing to release the need for my weight problem. I am willing to release the fear. I am willing to release the need for this protection. I am safe."

When we grow up, we have a tendency

to re-create the emotional environment

of our early home lives.

We tend to re-create relationships

we had with our mothers and fathers

or what they had between themselves.

I MAKE MY OWN DECISIONS

Many of you play power-struggle games with your parents. Parents push a lot of buttons. If you *want* to stop playing the games, you are going to actually *have to* stop playing the games.

It is time for you to grow up and decide what you want. You can begin by calling your parents by their first names. Start becoming three adults instead of two parents and a child.

It is safe to look within

for my peace of mind.

Each time you look deep into yourself,

you are going to find

incredibly beautiful treasures.

I AM AT THE CENTER OF PEACE

I affirm the following: The outer world does not touch me. I am in charge of my own being. I guard my inner world, for it is there that I create. I do whatever I need to do to keep my inner world peaceful. My inner peace is essential for my health and well-being. I go within and find that space where all is quiet and serene. I may see it as a peaceful, deep, quiet pool surrounded by green grass and tall, silent trees. I may feel it as white, billowy clouds upon which to lie and be caressed. I may hear it as flowing, delightful music soothing my senses.

No matter how I choose to experience my inner space, I find peace. At this center of peace, I am. I am the pureness and stillness of the center of my creative process. In peace, I create. In peace, I live and move and experience life. Because I keep myself centered in inner peace, I have peace in my outer world. Although others may have discord and chaos, it does not touch me, for I declare peace for myself. Although there may be madness all around me, I am calm and peaceful. The Universe is one of great order and peacefulness, and I reflect this in my every moment of life. The stars and the planets do not need to be worried or fearful in order to maintain their heavenly orbits. Nor does chaotic thinking contribute to my peaceful existence in life. I choose to express peacefulness, for I am peace. And so it is.

Start listening to what you say.

If you hear yourself using

negative or limiting words,

change them.

I SPEAK AND THINK POSITIVELY

If you could understand the power of your words, you would be careful about what you say. You would constantly use positive affirmations. The Universe always says *yes* to whatever you say, no matter what you choose to believe. If you choose to believe that you are not enough, and life will never be any good, and you will never get anything that you want, then the Universe will respond, and that is exactly what you will have.

The moment you start to change, the moment you are willing to bring good into your life, the Universe will respond in kind.

Each of us is doing

the very best we can at this moment.

If we knew better, if we had

more understanding and awareness,

we would do it differently.

But since we're doing our best,

we need to applaud ourselves

for our efforts.

I AM TOTALLY ADEQUATE AT ALL TIMES

Praise yourself and tell yourself how absolutely wonderful you are. Don't make yourself wrong. When you do something new, don't beat yourself up because you're not a pro at it the first time. Practice. Learn what does work and what doesn't work. Next time you do something new or different, something you are just learning, be there for yourself. Don't tell yourself what was wrong; tell yourself what was right with it.

Praise yourself. Build yourself up, so that the next time you do it, you really feel good about it. Each time you will be better and better and better. Soon you will have a new skill of some sort.

When we accept

the prosperity

that comes to us,

and are grateful for it,

even more will come to us.

I CONSTANTLY RECEIVE INCREDIBLE GIFTS

Learn to accept prosperity instead of exchanging it. If a friend gives you a gift or takes you to lunch, you don't have to immediately reciprocate. Allow the person to give you the gift. Accept it with joy and pleasure. You may never actually reciprocate with that person. You may give to someone else. If someone gives you a gift that you can't use or don't want, say: "I accept with pleasure and gratitude." And pass it on to someone else.

It's okay to be prosperous; there is no shame or guilt—just joy and acceptance.

We are all teachers and students.
Ask yourself: "What did I come here to
learn, and what did I come here to teach?"
Your loving relationships with others
will teach you more than
you could ever imagine.

ALL OF MY RELATIONSHIPS ARE ENVELOPED IN A CIRCLE OF LOVE

Envelop your family in a circle of love, whether they are living or not. Include your friends, your loved ones, your spouse, everyone from your work and your past, and all the people you would like to forgive and don't know how. Affirm that you have wonderful, harmonious relationships with everyone, where there is mutual respect and caring on both sides.

Know that you can live with dignity and peace and joy. Let this circle of love envelop the entire planet, and let your heart open so you have a space within you of unconditional love. You are worth loving. You are beautiful. You are powerful. And so it is.

Relax and enjoy life.

Know that whatever you need to know

is revealed to you in

the perfect time/space sequence.

I am at PEACE

Today you are a new person. Relax, and free your thoughts of all stresses and pressure. No person, place, or thing can irritate or annoy you. You are at peace. You are a free person living in a world that is a reflection of your own love and understanding. You are not *against* anything. You are *for* everything that will improve the quality of your life.

You use your words and thoughts as tools to shape your future. You express gratitude often, and look for things to be thankful for. You are relaxed. You live a peaceful life.

Take a nice, deep breath

and release your

negative patterns and habits.

And release the resistance to doing so.

I AM WILLING TO RELEASE THE NEED FOR THIS CONDITION

No matter how long your negative beliefs have been in your subconscious, affirm now that you are free of them. Affirm that you are willing to release the causes—the patterns in your consciousness that are creating negative conditions in your life. Affirm that you are now willing to release the need for these conditions. Know that they are disappearing, fading away, and dissolving back into the nothingness from whence they came.

The old garbage no longer has a hold on you. You are free!

You need to periodically

do some mental housecleaning

and toss out the rubbish

from the past—

the things that no longer suit you

or no longer fit you.

You want to polish those ideas

that are positive and good,

and use them more often.

I RELEASE THE PAST WITH EASE, AND I TRUST THE PROCESS OF LIFE

Close the door on old, painful memories. Close the door on old hurts, and old self-righteous unforgiveness. You might take an incident in the past where there was pain and hurt—something that is hard for you to forgive or look at. Ask yourself: "How long do I want to hold on to this? How long do I want to suffer because of something that happened in the past?"

Now see a stream in front of you and take this old experience—this hurt, this pain, this unforgiveness—and put the whole incident in the stream. See it begin to dissolve and drift downstream until it totally dissipates and disappears. You *do* have the ability to let go. You are free.

We resist most

that which we most need to learn.

If you keep saying "I can't" or "I won't,"

you are probably referring to

a lesson that is important to you.

I AM Wonderful, AND I AM PROUD OF MYSELF

Reprogramming your negative beliefs is very powerful. A good way to do so is by making a recording with your own voice on it. Record affirmations and play them back. They will have a great deal of value for you.

If you want a recording that is even more powerful, have your mother make one for you. Can you imagine going to sleep with your mother telling you how wonderful you are, how much she loves you, how proud she is of you, and how she knows you can be anything in this world?

Resentment, criticism, guilt, and fear

stem from blaming others

and not taking responsibility

for our own experiences.

I AM MOTIVATED BY LOVE

Release from within you all bitterness and resentment. Affirm that you are totally willing to freely forgive everyone. If you think of anyone who may have harmed you in any way at any point in your lifetime, bless that person with love and release him or her. Nobody can take anything from you that is rightfully yours. That which belongs to you will always return to you in Divine right order. If something does not come back to you, then it isn't meant to. Accept this with peace. Dissolving resentment is highly important. Trust yourself. You are safe. You are motivated by love.

It is very comfortable
to play the victim,
because then it is always
somebody else's fault.
You have to stand on your own two feet
and take some responsibility.

I HAVE THE POWER TO MAKE CHANGES

There is a difference between responsibility and blame. When we talk about responsibility, we are really talking about *having power*. When we talk about blame, we are talking about *making something or someone wrong*. Responsibility is a gift, because it gives you the power to make changes. Unfortunately, some choose to interpret it as guilt. These people usually accept everything as a guilt trip in one way or another because it is another way to make themselves wrong.

Being a victim is wonderful on one level, because then everyone else is responsible and we don't get a chance to make changes. When people insist on feeling guilty, there is not much we can do about it. They either accept the information or they don't. Just leave them alone. We are not responsible for their feeling guilty.

Some people don't know
how to say *no*.
The only way they know how
to say *no* is to be
ill or have accidents.
Know that it is okay to say *no*
to those things you
don't feel right about.
Trust yourself.

I AM FREE TO SAY NO IF SOMETHING ISN'T BEST FOR ME

If someone threw a hot potato at you, what would you do with it? Would you catch it? Would you hold it while it was burning your hand? Why would you even catch it? Why don't you just step out of the way? It is possible to refuse anything, even a gift. Are you aware of that?

You can say *no* to anything that doesn't feel right to you. You have the freedom and the power to do so. You can say *no* to invitations, presents, suggestions—anything! Use the power of your mind and your free will to do what you know is right.

We never get even.

Revenge does not work,

because what you give out

comes back to you.

The buck has to stop

somewhere.

I RELEASE ALL OLD HURTS AND FORGIVE MYSELF

When you hold on to the past with bitterness and anger and don't allow yourself to experience the present moment, you are wasting today. If you hold on to bitterness and grudges for a long time, it has to do with forgiving yourself, not the other person. If you hold on to old hurts, you punish yourself in the here and now. Often you sit in a prison of self-righteous resentment.

Do you want to be right, or do you want to be happy? Forgive yourself and stop punishing yourself.

Choose to believe that it is easy
to change a thought or a pattern.
It is your choice to do so.

I ALWAYS HAVE A CHOICE

Most of us have foolish ideas about who we are, and many rigid rules about how life *should* be lived. Let's remove the word *should* from our vocabulary forever. *Should* is a word that makes a prisoner of us. Every time we use *should*, we are making ourselves wrong or we are making someone else wrong. We are in effect saying "not good enough."

What can be dropped now from your *should* list? Replace the word *should* with the world *could*. *Could* lets you know that you have choice, and choice is freedom. We need to be aware that everything we do in life is done by choice. There is really nothing that we *have to* do. We always have a choice.

We need sleep to rejuvenate
the mind and spirit, as well
as the physical body.
We can release our
fears and problems
and just give in to
peaceful slumber.

I GIVE OVER, MY PROBLEMS AND SLEEP PEACEFULLY

Sleep is a time to restore ourselves and wrap up the day. Our bodies repair themselves and become renewed and refreshed. Our minds move into the dream state where the problems of the day are solved. We prepare ourselves for the new day ahead. As we enter the sleep state, we want to take positive thoughts with us— those that will create a wonderful new day and a wonderful new future. So if there is any anger or blame in you, let it go. If there is any resentment or fear, let it go. If there is any jealousy or rage, let it go. If there is any guilt or need for punishment lingering in the corners of your mind, let it go. Feel only peace in your mind and body as you drift off to sleep.

We create habits and problems
to fulfill a need within us.
When we can find a positive way
to fulfill the need,
we can release the problem.

THERE IS A SOLUTION TO EVERY PROBLEM

For every problem you create, there is a solution. You are not limited by your human-mind thinking, for you are connected with Universal Wisdom and Knowledge. You come from the loving space of your heart and know that love opens all doors. There is an ever-ready Power that helps you meet and overcome every challenge and crisis in your life. You know that every problem has been healed somewhere in the world. Therefore, you know that this can happen for you. You wrap yourself in a cocoon of love, and you are safe.

Every time you hear that something

is incurable, know in your mind

that it isn't true.

Know there is

an Infinite Healing Power.

INFINITE POWER IS ETERNAL

The sun is always shining. Even though clouds may come along and obscure the sun for a while, the sun is always shining. And even though the earth turns and the sun *appears* to go down, it really never stops shining. The same is true of Infinite Power and Infinite Spirit. It is eternal. It is healing. It is always here, always giving light to us. We may obscure its presence by the clouds of negative thinking, but that Spirit, that Power, that healing energy, is always with us.

In order to reprogram

the subconscious mind,

you need to relax the body.

Release the tension.

Let the emotions go.

Get to a state of openness and receptivity.

Think good things about yourself.

MY LIFE IS A JOY

Your subconscious mind does not know true from false or right from wrong. You never want to say something like "Oh, stupid old me," because the subconscious mind picks up on it; and after you say it for a while, you begin to feel that way. You begin to believe what you are saying. Don't joke about yourself, deprecate yourself, or make derogatory remarks about life, because that is not going to create good experiences for you.

When good comes into our lives

and we deny it by saying

"I don't believe it,"

we literally push our good away.

I DWELL ON POSITIVE THOUGHTS

Imagine that thoughts are like drops of water. When you think the same thoughts over and over again, you are creating this incredible body of water. First you have a little puddle, then you may get a pond, and as you continue to think the same thoughts over and over and over again, you have a lake and finally an ocean.

If your thoughts are negative, you can drown in a sea of your own negativity. If your thoughts are positive, you can float on the ocean of life.

The work you are doing on yourself

is not a goal, it is a process—

a lifetime process.

It doesn't matter how much time it takes—

you've got all the time in the world.

I am HERE AT THE RIGHT TIME

We are all on an endless journey through eternity, and the time we spend on this Earth plane is but a brief instant. We choose to come to this planet to learn lessons and to work on our spiritual growth and to expand our capacity to love. There is no right time and no wrong time to come and go. We always come in the middle of the movie, and we leave in the middle of the movie. We leave when our particular task is finished. We come to learn to love ourselves more and to share that love with all those around us. We come to open our hearts on a much deeper level. Our capacity to love is the only thing we take with us when we leave. If you left today, how much would you take?

If you don't trust other people,

it is because you are not there for yourself.

You don't support yourself.

You don't back yourself up.

When you really begin to be there for you,

then you will trust yourself;

and when you trust yourself,

you will trust other people.

I AM CONNECTED WITH A HIGHER POWER

Now is the time for you to learn about your own power and what you are capable of doing. What can you let go of? What can you nourish within you? What can you create? The wisdom and intelligence of the Universe is yours to use. Life is here to support you. If you get scared, think of your breath, and be aware of each breath as it goes in and out of your body. Your breath is the most precious substance you have, and it is so freely given to you. You have enough to last for as long as you shall live. If this most precious substance is so freely given that you can accept it without even thinking, can you not trust Life to supply you with the other things you need?

You are in the process

of becoming your own best friend—

the person you are most

happy to be with.

I LOVE and ACCEPT MYSELF ♥ RIGHT NOW

Many of you will not love yourselves until you lose weight, get a new job, find a new lover, or whatever. So you always put off loving yourself. What happens when you get the new job or the lover or you lose the weight . . . and you still don't love yourself? You just make another list and you have another waiting period. The only time you can begin to love who you are is right here and right now.

Unconditional love comes with no expectations. It is accepting what *is*.

When we grow up,

we get so worried about

what the neighbors think.

We ask ourselves,

"Will they approve of me?"

Everybody and everything is unique

and different and meant to be that way.

If we are like other people,

then we are not expressing

our own uniqueness.

I AM MY OWN UNIQUE SELF

You are not your father. You are not your mother. You are not any of your relatives. You are not your teachers at school, nor are you the limitations of your early religious training. You are *yourself*. You are special and unique, having your own set of talents and abilities. No one can do things exactly the way you can do them. There is no competition and no comparison.

You are worthy of your own love and your own self-acceptance. You are a magnificent being. You are free. Acknowledge this as the new truth for yourself. And so it is.

We are all on the cutting edge

of a profound awakening

of consciousness for the planet.

We can unite with our brothers and sisters

throughout the world

in unifying love.

I AM ONE WITH EVERYONE ON THE PLANET

There are not two conflicting powers—that is, good and evil. There is One Infinite Spirit, and there are human beings who have the opportunity to use the intelligence and wisdom and tools they have been given in every way. When you talk about *them,* you are talking about *us,* because we are the people, we are the government, we are the churches, and we are the planet.

The place to begin making changes is right where we are. It is all too easy to say: "It's the devil" or "It's them." It really is always *us!*

If you are going to listen to people,

listen to the winners.

Listen to those who know what

they are doing and who prove

what they are doing.

I AM a NATURAL WINNER

As we learn to love ourselves, we become powerful. Our love for ourselves moves us from being victims to being winners. Our love for ourselves attracts wonderful experiences to us. People who feel good about themselves are naturally attractive, because they have an aura about them that is just wonderful. They are always winning at Life. We can be willing to learn to love ourselves. We can be winners, too.

Work on doing what is right for you

and getting in touch with your own inner voice.

Your inner wisdom knows the

right answers for you.

I FOLLOW MY INNER WISDOM

Come from that wonderful, caring spot of your heart. Stay centered and love who you are. Know that you really are a Divine, Magnificent Expression of Life. No matter what is going on *out there,* you are centered. You have a right to your feelings. You have a right to your opinions. You just are. Work on loving yourself. Work on opening your heart. Sometimes it is scary to do that because the answers you get inside may be quite different from what your friends want you to do. Yet you know inwardly what is right for you. And if you follow this inner wisdom, you are at peace with your own being.

Support yourself in making the right choices for yourself. When you are in doubt, ask yourself: "Am I coming from the loving space of my heart? Is this a decision that is nurturing for me? Is this right for me now?" The decision you make at some later point—a day, a week, or a month later—may no longer be the right choice, and then you can change it. Ask in every moment: "Is this right for me?" And say: "I love myself and I am making the right choices."

When you release any negative thoughts
or feelings you have about work,
you find that each day becomes
a joy and an adventure.

I AM WORKING AT A CAREER THAT I REALLY ENJOY

What do you think about your work? Do you think of it as drudgery that you *have* to do, or do you see it as something you really love to do and enjoy? Begin to affirm that what you do is very fulfilling to you. You get pleasure from your work. You connect with the creativity of the Universe and allow it to flow through you in fulfilling ways. Affirm this every time negative thoughts come up about your work.

Everything in our lives is a mirror of us.

When something is happening at work

that isn't comfortable,

we have to look inside and say:

"How am I creating it?

What is within me that believes

I deserve this experience?"

I HAVE THE PERFECT WORKSPACE

I affirm the following: I see myself filled with gratitude and thanksgiving as I walk through this facility. I see the perfect space and equipment for mailing and shipping, the business offices laid out perfectly, an area just the right size for meetings. All the equipment needed is in its place; and the staff is made up of harmonious, dedicated people. The offices are beautiful, orderly, and peaceful.

I rejoice in the work being done to help, contribute to, or serve others. I see open, receptive souls drawn to the activities sponsored by this facility. I am thankful for the ever-flowing abundance that supports this mission. And so it is.

If you choose to believe

that everyone is working with you

in a productive and harmonious fashion,

you will find that wherever you go in life,

people are there to assist you.

WE ARE ALL PART OF THE harmonious whole

We are each a Divine idea expressing through the One Mind in harmonious ways. We have come together because there is something we need to learn from each other. We have a purpose in being together. There is no need to fight this purpose or to blame one another for what is happening. It is safe for us to work on loving ourselves so that we may benefit and grow from this experience. We choose to work together to bring harmony into the business at hand and into every area of our own lives. Everything we do is based on the one truth—the truth of our beings and the truth of Life.

Divine right action is guiding us every moment of the day. We say the right word at the right time and follow the right course of action at all times. Each person is part of the harmonious whole. There is a Divine blending of energies as people work joyfully together, supporting and encouraging each other in ways that are fulfilling and productive. We are successful in every area of our work and our lives. We are healthy, happy, loving, joyful, respectful, supportive, and at peace with ourselves and with each other. So be it, and so it is.

In this new time and this new age,

we are learning to go within

to find our savior.

We are the Power we are looking for.

Each one of us is totally linked

with the Universe and with Life.

THIS WORLD IS OUR HEAVEN ON EARTH

We are a community of spiritually minded souls who come together to share, grow, and radiate our energies into the world—each one free to pursue his or her activity and drawn together to better fulfill each individual's purpose. We are guided to form the new Heaven on Earth with others who have the same desire to prove to themselves and others that it can be now.

We live together harmoniously, lovingly, and peacefully—expressing God in our lives and in our living. We establish a world where the nurturing of soul growth is the most important activity, and where this is the work of the individual. There is ample time and opportunity for creative expression in whatever area we choose. All that we need we will be able to express through the powers within. There is no dis-ease, no poverty, no crime, and no deceit. The world of the future begins now, right here, with all of us. And so it is.

About the Author

Louise L. Hay, the author of the international bestseller *You Can Heal Your Life,* is a metaphysical lecturer and teacher with more than 50 million books sold worldwide. For more than 25 years, Louise has helped people throughout the world discover and implement the full potential of their own creative powers for personal growth and self-healing. She has appeared on *The Oprah Winfrey Show* and many other TV and radio programs both in the U.S. and abroad.

Louise is the founder and chairman of Hay House, Inc., which disseminates books, CDs, DVDs, and other products that contribute to the healing of the planet.

Websites: **www.LouiseHay.com**® and **www.HealYourLife.com**®.

My Own
Heart Thoughts

My Own
Heart Thoughts

My Own
Heart Thoughts

My Own
Heart Thoughts

My Own
Heart Thoughts

My Own
Heart Thoughts

My Own
Heart Thoughts

My Own
Heart Thoughts

My Own
Heart Thoughts

My Own
Heart Thoughts

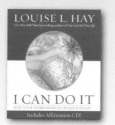

We hope you enjoyed this Hay House Lifestyles book.
If you'd like to receive our online catalog featuring additional information
on Hay House books and products, or if you'd like to find out more
about the Hay Foundation, please contact:

Hay House, Inc., P.O. Box 5100, Carlsbad, CA 92018-5100
(760) 431-7695 or (800) 654-5126
(760) 431-6948 (fax) or (800) 650-5115 (fax)
www.hayhouse.com® • **www.hayfoundation.org**

Published and distributed in Australia by: Hay House Australia Pty. Ltd., 18/36 Ralph St.,
Alexandria NSW 2015 • *Phone:* 612-9669-4299 • *Fax:* 612-9669-4144 • www.hayhouse.com.au

Published and distributed in the United Kingdom by: Hay House UK, Ltd., 292B Kensal Rd.,
London W10 5BE • *Phone:* 44-20-8962-1230 • *Fax:* 44-20-8962-1239 • www.hayhouse.co.uk

Published and distributed in the Republic of South Africa by: Hay House SA (Pty), Ltd., P.O. Box
990, Witkoppen 2068 • *Phone/Fax:* 27-11-467-8904 • www.hayhouse.co.za

Published in India by: Hay House Publishers India, Muskaan Complex, Plot No. 3, B-2, Vasant Kunj,
New Delhi 110 070 • *Phone:* 91-11-4176-1620 • *Fax:* 91-11-4176-1630 • www.hayhouse.co.in

Distributed in Canada by: Raincoast, 9050 Shaughnessy St., Vancouver, B.C. V6P 6E5 •
Phone: (604) 323-7100 • *Fax:* (604) 323-2600 • www.raincoast.com

Take Your Soul on a Vacation

Visit **www.HealYourLife.com**® to regroup, recharge, and reconnect
with your own magnificence. Featuring blogs, mind-body-spirit news,
and life-changing wisdom from Louise Hay and friends.

Visit **www.HealYourLife.com** today!